# 萨卡加维亚

Heroes and Role Models | Non-Fiction Series

Copyright © 2022 by Level Learning, INC. and Washington Yu Ying PCS™
Original and Edited Text Copyright © 2022 by Washington Yu Ying PCS™

All rights reserved. No part of this book in whole or part may be reproduced without written permission from the publisher.

Published by Level Learning, INC.

Content Contributors:
Washington Yu Ying PCS™
Level Learning - Ya-Ching Chang

Illustrations by: Josh Taira

Leveling classification based on Level Learning standard. For full description, visit www.levellearning.com

ISBN 978-1-64040-003-0
*Simplified Chinese Edition*

**About Level Learning:**
Level Learning provides a literacy focused curriculum specifically designed for K-12 Chinese as a Second Language classrooms. Our program offers 20 levels of specific and detailed objectives, leveled texts and passages, mastery-based online assessment, and analytics to enable data-driven instruction. Level Learning reading curriculum for both literature and informational text emphasize grammar and comprehension skills to help teachers develop confident and independent Chinese language readers. The non-fiction series of books are specifically designed to support our informational text course based on multiple national standards. To learn more about our entire offering, visit www.levellearning.com.

**About Washington Yu Ying PCS™:**
Washington Yu Ying PCS is a Mandarin English dual language immersion International Baccalaureate (IB) World school. Yu Ying's mission is to inspire and prepare young people to create a better world by challenging them to reach their full potential in a nurturing Chinese/English educational environment. Yu Ying's comprehensive IB, dual immersion curriculum equips students with global competencies for success in the real world. As a leader in immersion education, Yu Ying is determined to advance Chinese language programs and global citizenry education by helping other schools create and strengthen their Chinese programs. For more information, email: products@washingtonyuying.org

你知道萨卡加维亚的故事吗?萨卡加维亚出生于1788年。她是美国**原住民**,也是一位**著名**的远征者。

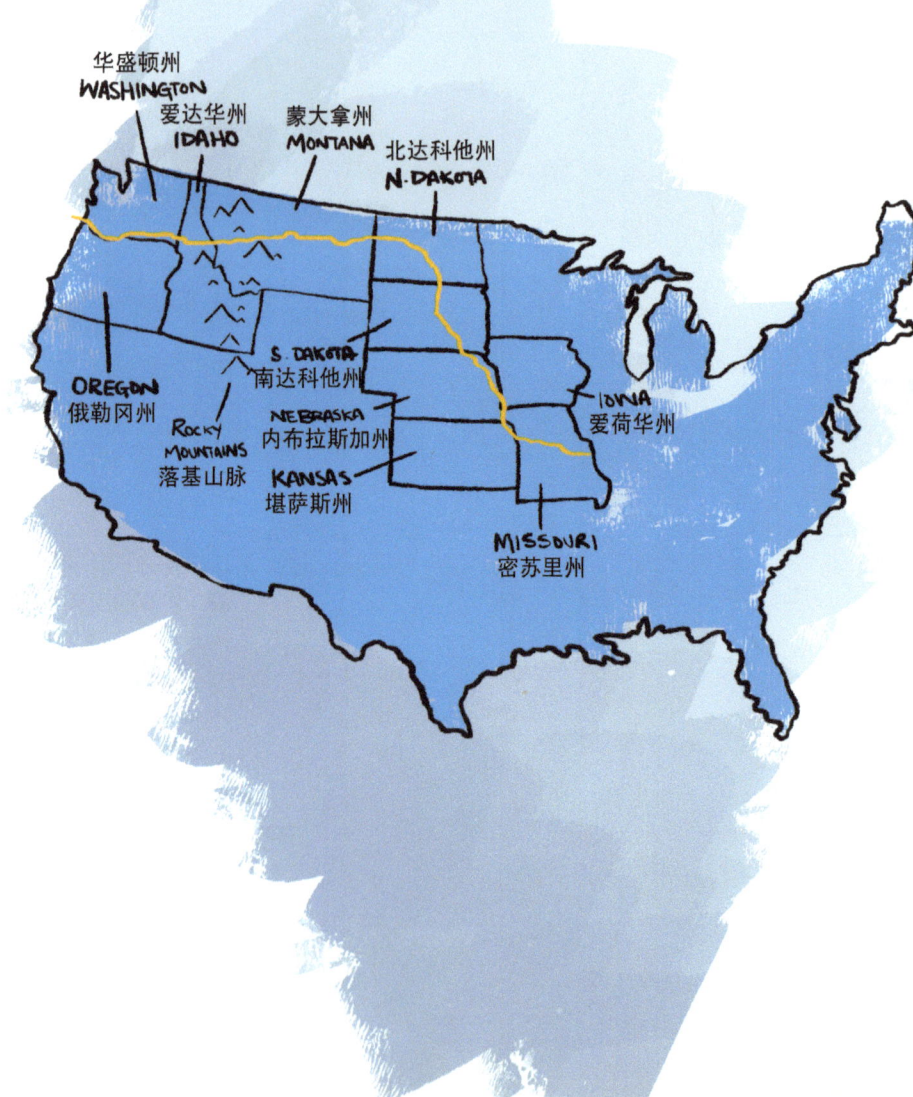

有一天，萨卡加维亚住的村子里来了一支远征队。路易斯和克拉克带着这支远征队，想要前往美国西部。因为他们不会说原住民语，所以需要村民的帮助。

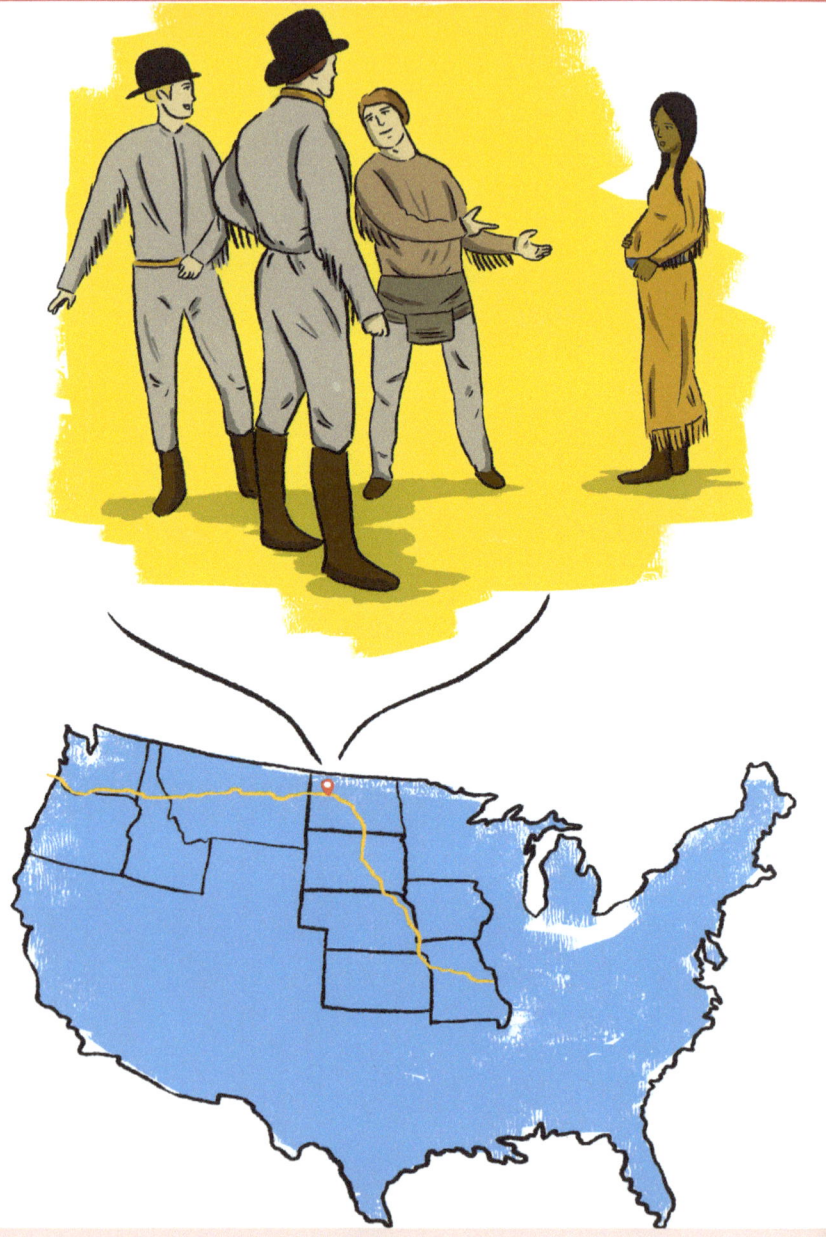

萨卡加维亚会说原住民语。路易斯和克拉克知道以后,希望她可以加入远征队。那时候,怀孕的萨卡加维亚快要生宝宝了。

不久后,萨卡加维亚就生下了一个宝宝。为了帮助路易斯和克拉克,她便带着宝宝加入了远征队。

前往西部的路上,天气非常寒冷。大家经常又冷又饿,没有东西吃。萨卡加维亚教大家采集可以吃的植物和果实。

除此之外，萨卡加维亚还帮忙带路和翻译。路上的原住民看到了女人和宝宝，都对远征队非常友善。路易斯和克拉克相信萨卡加维亚和宝宝为大家带来了和平。

有了萨卡加维亚的帮助，这次的远征非常顺利。远征队到达了美国西部，也见到了太平洋。

在2000年，美国发行了一枚新的硬币。硬币上有萨卡加维亚带宝宝远征的画像。这枚硬币是用来纪念萨卡加维亚对远征的帮助。

# Glossary

|  | Pinyin | English Definition |
|---|---|---|
| 原住民 | yuán zhù mín | natives |
| 著名 | zhù míng | famous |
| 村子 | cūn zi | village |
| 远征队 | yuǎn zhēng duì | expedition team |
| 前往 | qián wǎng | to go |
| 西部 | xī bù | west |
| 原住民语 | yuán zhù mín yǔ | native language |
| 需要 | xū yào | to need |
| 村民 | cūn mín | villagers |
| 帮助 | bāng zhù | help |
| 加入 | jiā rù | to join |
| 怀孕 | huái yùn | pregnant |
| 寒冷 | hán lěng | cold |
| 采集 | cǎi jí | to collect, to gather |
| 植物 | zhí wù | plant |

|  | Pinyin | English Definition |
|---|---|---|
| 果实 | guǒ shí | fruit |
| 带路 | dài lù | to guide the way |
| 翻译 | fān yì | to translate |
| 友善 | yǒu shàn | friendly |
| 相信 | xiāng xìn | to believe |
| 和平 | hé píng | peace |
| 顺利 | shùn lì | smoothly |
| 到达 | dào dá | to reach, to arrive |
| 太平洋 | tài píng yáng | Pacific Ocean |
| 发行 | fā xíng | to issue |
| 硬币 | yìng bì | coin |
| 画像 | huà xiàng | portrait |
| 纪念 | jì niàn | to commemorate, to remember |

www.ingramcontent.com/pod-product-compliance
Lightning Source LLC
Chambersburg PA
CBHW041225070526
44584CB00001B/96